"Equipped with his five senses,
man explores the universe around him
and calls the adventure Science."
—Edwin Hubble

"Women, like men, should try
to do the impossible."
—Amelia Earhart

"I have learned to use the word impossible
with the greatest caution."
—Wernher von Braun

BUZZ ALDRIN
Look to the Stars

Paintings by WENDELL MINOR

G. P. PUTNAM'S SONS

To the Stargazers who chart the galaxies,

And the Rocketeers who build flying spaceships.

To the Astronauts who dare to explore,

And the Global Space Travelers who venture outward.

To yearning explorers, past, present and future—

Let us always *look to the stars*.

—Buzz Aldrin

To a new generation of young explorers. May you learn from those who have gone before.

—Wendell Minor

Wendell Minor wishes to acknowledge the NASA image collection and the Johnson Space Center collection for their valuable reference sources, Dr. Buzz Aldrin for his critical eye in aiding the artist, and Walter Myers, computer graphic artist at arcadiastreet.com, for his expert help in creating reference images that depict our future in space. Please refer to the selected reading list and websites in the back of this book, which were also of great help in gathering additional visual and factual information.

G. P. PUTNAM'S SONS A division of Penguin Young Readers Group. Published by The Penguin Group. Penguin Group (USA) Inc., 375 Hudson Street, New York, NY 10014, U.S.A. Penguin Group (Canada), 90 Eglinton Avenue East, Suite 700, Toronto, Ontario M4P 2Y3, Canada (a division of Pearson Penguin Canada Inc.). Penguin Books Ltd, 80 Strand, London WC2R 0RL, England. Penguin Ireland, 25 St. Stephen's Green, Dublin 2, Ireland (a division of Penguin Books Ltd.). Penguin Group (Australia), 250 Camberwell Road, Camberwell, Victoria 3124, Australia (a division of Pearson Australia Group Pty Ltd). Penguin Books India Pvt Ltd, 11 Community Centre, Panchsheel Park, New Delhi - 110 017, India. Penguin Group (NZ), 67 Apollo Drive, Rosedale, North Shore 0632, New Zealand (a division of Pearson New Zealand Ltd). Penguin Books (South Africa) (Pty) Ltd, 24 Sturdee Avenue, Rosebank, Johannesburg 2196, South Africa. Penguin Books Ltd, Registered Offices: 80 Strand, London WC2R 0RL, England.

The art was done in gouache watercolor on Strathmore 500 bristol, 4 ply.

Library of Congress Cataloging-in-Publication Data

Aldrin, Buzz. Look to the stars / Buzz Aldrin ; paintings by Wendell Minor. p. cm. 1. Astronautics—Juvenile literature. 2. Interplanetary voyages—Juvenile literature. 3. Space flights—Juvenile literature. 4. Outer space—Exploration—Juvenile literature. 5. Aldrin, Buzz—Juvenile literature. I. Minor, Wendell, ill. II. Title. TL793.A435 2009 629.409—dc22 2008018575

ISBN 978-0-399-24721-7

1 3 5 7 9 10 8 6 4 2

CONTENTS

INTRODUCTION

Since the beginning of time, humans have looked to the moon and the stars with great wonder. Some even dreamed of traveling into space—I know I did! But space travel was still science fiction during my childhood; only comic book heroes like Flash Gordon and Buck Rogers blasted off into space. Going to the moon or Mars was something only they could do, or so we thought.

When I was a boy, I admired my dad's achievements as a pilot. Our house was filled with photos from many of his friends who were among the great aviation pioneers of their time—including a picture of the Wright brothers signed by Orville Wright and a signed picture of Amelia Earhart christening the two-engine amphibian plane that my dad flew for Standard Oil of New Jersey. I flew in that very plane at the age of six! My dad's love of flying became my inspiration to look to the stars.

2009 marks the fortieth anniversary of Apollo 11, when Neil Armstrong, Mike Collins, and I traveled to the moon. Neil and I were the first to walk on its surface. Let's look back to where this journey began, and then look forward to where it might lead.

Buzz Aldrin

My dad, Edwin Aldrin Sr., was a young Army aviator in 1923

A NEW VIEW OF THE UNIVERSE

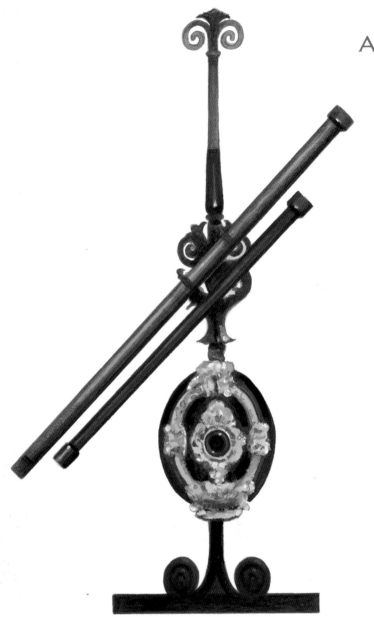

Galileo's telescope

When searching the night sky as a boy, I often wondered about the first people to study the stars. When Nicolaus Copernicus was a boy, people believed that the Earth was the center of our solar system. Copernicus had a different idea. He said that the Earth was a planet that revolved around the sun.

Galileo was the first astronomer to observe the planets through a telescope, and what he saw convinced him that Copernicus was right. He also observed the Earth's moon and saw craters and mountains there.

German astronomer and scientist Johannes Kepler even dreamed about traveling to the moon! Kepler's laws of motion proved that the orbits of the planets were elliptical, not round.

And what about Isaac Newton? He invented the reflecting telescope and advanced the laws of motion and gravity. As strange as it may seem, Newton found that the force causing an apple to fall to the ground is the same force that holds the moon and planets in their orbits! It was Newton's theory of gravity that established the basic foundation for advancement in manned powered flight.

Isaac Newton

FIRST FLIGHTS!

As boys, Orville and Wilbur Wright built kites and dreamed of flying someday. After years of hard work, their dreams came true when these two young bicycle builders from Dayton, Ohio, finally did what no one had ever done before.

On a cold and windy morning in December 1903, Orville flew the *Wright Flyer 1* a distance of 120 feet in 12 seconds. True, that's not a long time, but what an exciting 12 seconds! Then brother Wilbur took the controls later that day, flying 852 feet in 59 seconds. The heavier-than-air flying machine had lifted from the sandy beaches of Kitty Hawk, North Carolina—and into history. This was the beginning of the aviation era.

Spirit of St. Louis

Charles Lindbergh made history too with the first solo transatlantic flight in 1927—from Long Island, New York, to Paris, France. His small single-engine plane, *Spirit of St. Louis,* covered the 3,610 miles in 33.5 hours. The farm boy's dream of flying had become one more giant step for manned flight.

In 1969, only sixty-six years after the Wright brothers' first successful flight of the *Wright Flyer 1*, Neil Armstrong and I landed on the moon with a piece of fabric from that very same plane.

I think Orville and Wilbur would have been pleased—and very proud.

VISIONS OF OTHER WORLDS

I believe you must challenge yourself to think big and believe that anything is possible. Astronomer Edwin Hubble and physics professor Robert Goddard did just that. Edwin Hubble was the first person to discover galaxies beyond our own. He also proved that our universe is constantly expanding. His quest to observe and understand the distant stars was inspired by Jules Verne's 1865 novel *From the Earth to the Moon*.

Young Robert Goddard was also inspired by reading science fiction. As a teenager he read H. G. Wells' *War of the Worlds* and dreamed of inventing a machine that would take humans to the moon and to Mars. On a wintry March day in 1926, Goddard successfully launched the first liquid-fueled rocket in history. Zoom! Although his rocket flew only 184 feet to an altitude of 41 feet in 2.5 seconds, its launch really signaled the birth of the space age.

My dad studied under Dr. Goddard, and I believe his friendships with his teacher and Charles Lindbergh helped advance aviation and space science. Dad arranged a meeting between his two friends and Lindbergh helped find support for Goddard's research, which set the stage for bigger and better rockets to come.

Mount Wilson Observatory

"The great spirals . . . apparently lie outside our stellar system."—Edwin Hubble

*Robert Goddard's first rocket flight
at his Aunt Effie's farm*

BREAKING NEW BARRIERS

It amazes me that I have had the good fortune to know and work with many of the great contributors to aviation science and history.

Wernher von Braun

As a child, Wernher von Braun wanted to travel to the moon. When he was eighteen, von Braun joined a rocket society in Berlin to pursue his dream. Years later, he helped develop and launch the V-2 rocket (Vengeance-2) for the German Army in World War II, applying Dr. Goddard's basic design for liquid fuel propulsion.

The V-2 had a speed of 3,500 miles per hour and could travel a distance of 250 miles. After the war, von Braun fled to America, where his V-2 rocket would eventually be developed into the Redstone rocket that put the first American into space.

Captain Chuck Yeager, the famous World War II fighter ace, became the first human to break the sound barrier in the Bell X-1 rocket plane. This gigantic sonic boom was a major breakthrough for flight that many thought impossible to achieve.

Later, my future Apollo 11 commander, Neil Armstrong, set many speed and altitude records in the hypersonic X-15 research plane, which provided important information for flight above the Earth's atmosphere.

V-2 rocket

"Basic research is what I am doing when I don't know what I am doing."—Wernher von Braun

Bell X-1 rocket plane

NASA's X-15

Neil Armstrong

"Research is creating new knowledge."—Neil Armstrong

"We Were First"—Russian newspaper headline, October 4, 1957

MESSAGES FROM SPACE

I first heard the beeps on the radio and somehow knew that the world had changed forever. The small, shiny, silver sphere called *Sputnik* was only about the size of a basketball. It had four long antennae that transmitted a beeping radio signal back to Earth. On radios around the world, you could tune in to hear the beeps. It seemed to many people like pure science fiction! But it was far from that.

This was the first time a man-made satellite could communicate from space to Earth—amazing!

When the Soviet Union put *Sputnik* into orbit in 1957, the great space race with the United States was off and running.

America successfully launched its first satellite, *Explorer 1*, into orbit in 1958, the very same year that NASA—the National Aeronautics and Space Administration—was established.

Nearly every child in America looked to the night sky to search for the tiny, moving "stars" that were the first satellites. Those satellites inspired a new generation of children to study math and science to prepare for future careers in space exploration.

THE FIRST ASTRONAUTS

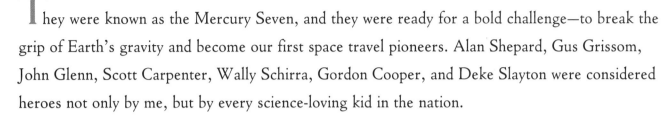

They were known as the Mercury Seven, and they were ready for a bold challenge—to break the grip of Earth's gravity and become our first space travel pioneers. Alan Shepard, Gus Grissom, John Glenn, Scott Carpenter, Wally Schirra, Gordon Cooper, and Deke Slayton were considered heroes not only by me, but by every science-loving kid in the nation.

America was rushing to catch up again with Russia, who had just put the first man in space. Cosmonaut Yuri Gagarin orbited the Earth once in 1961. Twenty-three days after Gagarin's flight, Alan Shepard climbed into the tiny, cramped Mercury 3 capsule, *Freedom 7*. The spacecraft measured just 6 feet 10 inches in length and 6 feet 3 inches in diameter—not much bigger than a go-kart! Wernher von Braun's Redstone rocket was used to launch *Freedom 7*. Alan Shepard became the first American in space, and although he didn't orbit the Earth, Shepard reached an altitude of over 116 miles during his 15-minute flight. Americans cheered when they heard Mission Control say, "Everything is A-OK!"

Yuri Gagarin

After Shepard's success, President John F. Kennedy challenged America, saying, "I believe that this nation should commit itself to achieving the goal, before this decade is out, of landing a man on the moon and returning him safely to the Earth." It seemed impossible, and even more impossible that I would eventually participate in that goal!

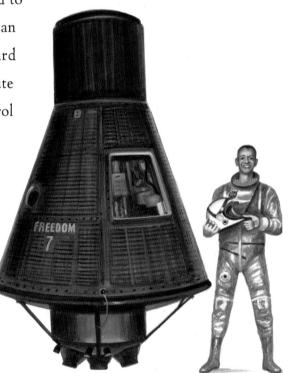

Astronaut Alan Shepard and his Freedom 7 *capsule*

"I could have gone on flying through space forever."—Yuri Gagarin

"I don't know what you could say about a day in which you have seen four beautiful sunsets."—John Glenn Jr.

In 1962, Astronaut John Glenn climbed aboard his *Friendship 7* capsule perched on top of the new Atlas rocket, which was almost five times more powerful than the Redstone. I was one of millions of Americans who watched on television as Glenn blasted off into space. He became the first American to orbit the Earth—not once, but three times! It wasn't a snap either. After the first orbit, his autopilot failed, so Glenn had to take over the manual controls for the remaining two orbits to complete his mission. This incident proved how important it was to have manual controls in case the autopilot failed.

The reentry of Friendship 7

During Project Mercury's final mission, Gordon Cooper spent thirty-four hours orbiting the Earth and was the first man to spend a night in space. When it was time to return, he too was forced to take over the manual controls since the automated reentry system wasn't working properly. Cooper piloted his craft to a perfect reentry. The six Mercury missions proved that humans could function in space and return safely.

At the time, I was studying astronautics and developing orbital rendezvous techniques at the Massachusetts Institute of Technology. The year after earning my doctorate degree, I was accepted into the third group of NASA astronauts. I felt I was on my way—up!

John Glenn Jr. boards Friendship 7

Speaking of the Mercury Seven astronauts: "We're kind of like a bunch of brothers. We're quite close."—Gordon Cooper

19

Astronaut Ed White takes America's first space walk

After his space walk Ed White said,
"I felt red, white and blue all over."

GEMINI—BRIDGE TO THE MOON

One of Project Gemini's goals was to keep humans in space for up to two weeks—even though the Gemini spacecraft had no more room than the front seats of a Volkswagen Beetle!

The Gemini astronauts were the first to rendezvous and dock two vehicles in space and venture outside of a spacecraft. My friend Ed White from West Point was the first American to walk in space.

The most amazing Gemini mission of all was perhaps Gemini 8, when Neil Armstrong and Dave Scott accomplished the first docking with an unmanned spacecraft. Disaster seemed certain when the two joined vehicles began to tumble out of control because a rocket thruster got stuck in the "on" position, but Neil managed to undock, manually regain control of their craft, and make an emergency landing. By doing this, Neil not only saved the mission—he saved their lives!

I had the privilege of being on board the final Gemini mission, Gemini 12, with my friend Jim Lovell. We completed rendezvous and docking with our target vehicle twice, and I perfected pressure-suited maneuvering techniques while making world-record space walks totaling five hours and thirty-two minutes.

America's space program was on a roll. We were now ready to shoot for the moon with Project Apollo.

Gemini capsule scale to astronauts

During my space walk I said, "Jim, I'm gonna clean your windshield."
Jim Lovell responded, "Hey Buzz, check the oil too, would ya?"

21

PROJECT APOLLO: THE DREAM COMES TRUE

When Neil Armstrong and I touched down on the moon's surface in the *Eagle*, we fulfilled President Kennedy's challenge. We had won the race to the moon, and the whole world watched and cheered. Even a science fiction writer like Jules Verne could not have imagined a spaceship taller than a 36-story building, more powerful than 100,000 locomotives, and weighing more than 6 million pounds.

Think of it. Six moon landings in only four years. Just twelve men have ever actually walked on the moon, and believe me when I say I am proud to be one of them.

Nearly 400,000 dedicated people worked on Project Apollo, and I thank them, one and all! It's no exaggeration to call Apollo the most spectacular scientific triumph of the twentieth century. The dreams of Copernicus, Galileo, Kepler, Newton, Goddard, von Braun, and so many more had finally come true!

To be a space pioneer, you have to be willing to risk everything, possibly even your life. Project Apollo began with the tragic loss of my Air Force squadron mate, Ed White, and his crewmates Roger Chaffee and Gus Grissom. The Apollo 1 capsule fire on Launch Pad 34 in 1967 shocked and saddened all Americans. As a result of that accident, NASA redesigned the Apollo's capsule to ensure the safety of future astronauts. I believe all the Apollo crews that followed owe a debt of gratitude to these courageous men.

"That's one small step for [a] man, one giant leap for mankind."—Neil Armstrong

"Beautiful, beautiful. Magnificent desolation."—Buzz Aldrin

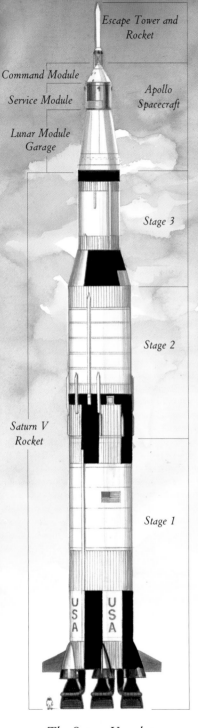

Escape Tower and Rocket

Command Module

Service Module

Apollo Spacecraft

Lunar Module Garage

Stage 3

Stage 2

Saturn V Rocket

Stage 1

USA   USA

The Saturn V rocket was 363 feet tall

THE AMAZING APOLLO MISSIONS

The three-stage Saturn V rocket that launched the Apollo missions was a design marvel created by Wernher von Braun and his NASA team. It was made up of over three million parts! The first stage's engines burned at liftoff, after which the whole stage was discarded. Then the second and third stages kicked in and were discarded after their fuel was burned.

The Apollo spacecrafts sat atop this powerful rocket for their historic journeys into space.

THE MISSIONS AT A GLANCE

Apollo 7 / Oct. 11–22, 1968
Astronauts Schirra, Eisele and Cunningham
First manned Apollo spacecraft tested in Earth orbit
First live TV broadcast from space

"Houston, Apollo. I've got the world in my window."—Michael Collins, command module pilot

Apollo 8 / Dec. 21–27, 1968

Astronauts Borman, Lovell and Anders
First manned flight of the Saturn V rocket
First manned lunar orbit
First images of earthrise over the moon
Live TV broadcast on Christmas Eve

Apollo 9 / March 3–13, 1969

Astronauts McDivitt, Scott and Schweickart
First manned flight of all lunar hardware
 in Earth orbit
First rendezvous of lunar module

Apollo 10 / May 18–26, 1969

Command module: Charlie Brown
Lunar lander: Snoopy
Astronauts Stafford, Young and Cernan
First dress rehearsal for moon landing
First live color TV broadcast from space

Apollo 11 / July 16–24, 1969

Command module: Columbia
Lunar lander: Eagle
Astronauts Armstrong, Collins and Aldrin
First manned lunar landing in history:
 "Houston, Tranquility Base here. The *Eagle*
 has landed." —Neil Armstrong, July 20, 1969
Neil and Buzz collect the first moon rocks

Apollo 12 / Nov. 14–24, 1969

Command module: Yankee Clipper
Lunar lander: Intrepid
Astronauts Conrad, Gordon and Bean
75 pounds of moon material collected
Brought back items from *Surveyor 3* spacecraft

Apollo 13 / April 11–17, 1970

Command module: Odyssey
Lunar lander: Aquarius
Astronauts Lovell, Swigert and Haise
Oxygen tank explosion in the service module
 aborted the landing mission
The dedication of Mission Control and
 the astronauts saved the day

Apollo 14 / Jan. 31–Feb. 9, 1971

Command module: Kitty Hawk
Lunar lander: Antares
Astronauts Shepard, Roosa and Mitchell
Handcart used for the first time to collect rocks
94 pounds of moon material collected

Apollo 15 / July 26–Aug. 7, 1971

Command module: Endeavor
Lunar lander: Falcon
Astronauts Scott, Worden and Irwin
First use of lunar rover
169 pounds of moon material collected

Apollo 16 / April 16–27, 1972

Command module: Casper
Lunar lander: Orion
Astronauts Young, Mattingly and Duke
First study of the lunar highlands area
209 pounds of moon material collected

Apollo 17 / Dec. 7–19, 1972

Command module: America
Lunar lander: Challenger
Astronauts Cernan, Evans and Schmitt
First scientist-astronaut to land on the moon
243 pounds of moon material collected

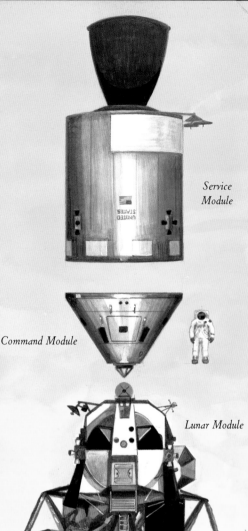

Service Module

Command Module

Lunar Module

Apollo Spacecraft

An Apollo spacecraft was made up of three separate modules:
 The **command module** was the control center and housed a crew of three astronauts.
 The **service module** contained the life-support systems for the crew, as well as a source of reusable rocket power for the journey.
 The **lunar module** carried two astronauts to the moon's surface and was housed for launch in the LM adapter (lunar module garage).

After all of our successful Apollo missions, NASA turned its attention to the challenges of living in space for long periods of time by launching Skylab, America's first orbiting laboratory, in 1973. Twenty-five years after the launch of Skylab, construction began on the International Space Station. The ISS is the largest research facility ever to be built in space—a permanent orbiting platform where astronauts from many countries learn how to live and work "off planet." It is scheduled to be completed by 2010.

I believe the ISS will continue to be a gateway to new frontiers where scientists can study the effects of weightlessness and conduct experiments to learn how humans might live in space not for months, but years.

Skylab

Astronauts and cosmonauts met in space for the first time when an Apollo command module docked with a Russian Soyuz craft in 1975

"Space is our frontier and beginning its exploration may be our generation's greatest contribution to human history."
—Alan Bean

The International Space Station
nears completion in 2010

October 2007, two women meet in space—Space Shuttle Discovery Commander Pamela Melroy and
ISS Commander Peggy Whitson

THE SPACE SHUTTLE

What launches like a rocket and lands like plane? It's the space shuttle, of course. It is the most complicated spaceship ever built, with more than two and a half million parts, and weighing over four and a half million pounds at launch. It can carry up to seven astronauts and 35,000 pounds of cargo, and was designed to be flown again and again. In more than one hundred missions, the crews of the spaceships *Challenger*, *Columbia*, *Discovery*, *Atlantis* and *Endeavour* have achieved amazing things. They have delivered and repaired communications and weather satellites, and transported large sections of the International Space Station. And don't forget the famous Hubble Space Telescope—the shuttle was the only space vehicle large enough to deliver it to space. And when Hubble needed repair, a shuttle crew was sent to fix it. With satellites beaming down images from Hubble, you can view amazing pictures of the universe on your computer screen with just a few clicks. The fleet of shuttles is scheduled to be retired in 2010 after delivering the final sections of the International Space Station.

"Having the opportunity to fly the first flight of something like a space shuttle was the ultimate test flight."—Robert Cripp

Hubble Space Telescope

There is, though, a sad side to this story. Two shuttle missions have had tragic accidents. I, along with the rest of the world, mourned when all of the astronauts were lost aboard Challenger in 1986 and Columbia in 2003. We will always remember those who risked their lives to advance our knowledge of science. Christa McAuliffe, the "first teacher in space," is an everlasting reminder of that sacrifice. I will never forget her inspiring message: "I touch the future. I teach." And we continue to learn.

THE ROAD BACK TO THE MOON

Our first return missions to the moon will be unmanned probes in preparation for human missions sometime around 2020. Scientists believe we will be able to extract oxygen and water from the moon's craters and harness the sun's rays into electricity. Astronauts will do this work with the help of robots, which will make it possible to have a manned base on the moon.

Someday, I believe there will be a large lunar station that will be in a permanent orbit around the Earth, up near the moon. This space station will become a stopover for space travelers on their way to the moon and beyond.

Just as Lewis and Clark journeyed west into the unknown in 1803 to discover a new world, you will be part of a generation of explorers who will discover new worlds beyond our own. Are you ready?

We will establish "a new foothold on the moon, and . . . new journeys to worlds beyond our own."
—President George W. Bush, 2004

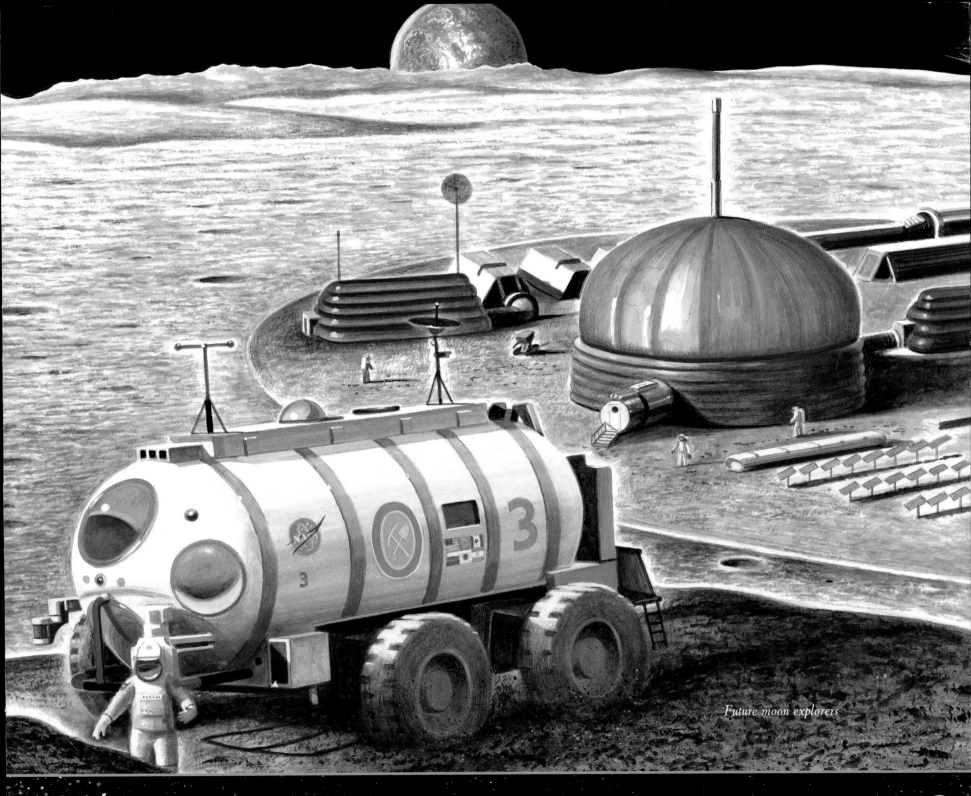

Future moon explorers

"Using the space station and building an outpost on the moon to prepare for the trip to Mars are critical milestones in America's quest . . ."—Michael Griffin, NASA

31

FIRST ROBOTS,
THEN HUMANS TO MARS!

Space probes have given us a fascinating look at many of the planets in our solar system. The Cassini/Huygens probe is orbiting Saturn, and the New Horizons probe will fly past Pluto in 2015. *Voyager 1* and *2* journeyed to Jupiter, Saturn, Uranus and Neptune, and *Voyager 1* has been traveling in space for more than 30 years. It will be the first probe to go beyond our solar system.

Because of probes such as *Viking, Pathfinder,* and the Mars rovers, we know a great deal about our closest planetary neighbor. We know that Mars has giant volcanoes and great canyons under its hazy pink sky. We know there was once water on its surface. Where did this water come from? Why is it no longer there? Maybe there were once simple life-forms on the mysterious red planet. We will go and find the answers!

I foresee manned missions to Mars using a reusable spacecraft that will cycle continually between Earth and Mars in permanent orbit. Astronauts will board a "taxi" spacecraft from Earth to rendezvous with the Aldrin Mars Cycler for the trip to the red planet. The cycler's continual trips could make it possible to establish Mars as our second home someday soon, with a permanent human presence.

Mars rover Spirit
explores the red planet

The future Aldrin Mars Cycler might look something like this

"The rovers are amazing machines, and they continue to produce amazing . . . results."—Alan Stern, NASA

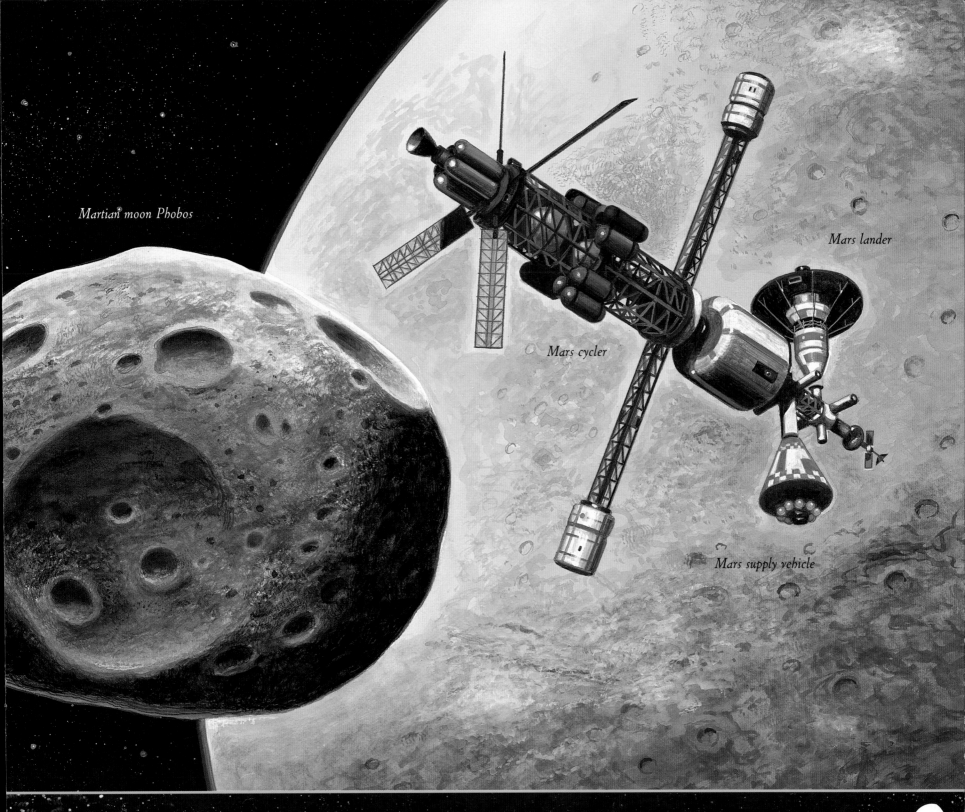

Martian moon Phobos

Mars cycler

Mars lander

Mars supply vehicle

"Mars is there, waiting to be reached." —Buzz Aldrin

YOUR FUTURE IN SPACE

You may never become an astronaut, but it doesn't mean you won't be able to visit space. You may not think so, but space tourism will likely become a reality in your lifetime. Try this for a special holiday: Take a space "tour bus" or visit an Earth-orbiting "hotel." Imagine the games you can play in zero gravity! Maybe you'll choose to take a trip swinging around the moon to see the earthrise as you come around the far side, just as Apollo 8's crew did on Christmas Eve in 1968. One day your family may have some amazing vacation choices. Where will you go? Will it be to the seashore on Earth, or to the moon's Sea of Tranquility?

SpaceShipOne

My ShareSpace Foundation is committed to educating young people about careers in science and space travel for private citizens. A space lottery will make it possible for almost anyone to win an adventure-award trip on a future tour. Will you perhaps get a winning number? Wouldn't it be fantastic to see the wonders of our home planet from space, just as I did? In one way, it's already started. Many private citizens around the globe are now working on inventing spacecraft designs for commercial use. Burt Rutan and his team designed and built *SpaceShipOne*, the first privately developed piloted craft to enter the realm of space. Who will be the Wright brothers of the twenty-first century? A new space race is on!

AFTERWORD

Forty years have come and gone with amazing speed since the day Neil Armstrong and I first put our footprints in that powdery moondust on July 20, 1969.

When I gave my speech on Capitol Hill in Washington, D.C., after our historic mission, I said: "We walked on the moon. But the footprints at Tranquility Base belong to more than the crew of Apollo 11. They were put there by hundreds of thousands of people across this country. . . . And since we came in peace for all mankind, those footprints belong also to all the people of the world. . . . The first step on the moon was a step toward our sister planets and ultimately toward the stars. 'A small step for a man,' was a statement of fact, 'a giant leap for mankind,' is a hope for the future." It was my hope then, and it is still my hope today. I remember the words of my father's teacher, Dr. Robert Goddard: "It is difficult to say what is impossible, for the dream of yesterday is the hope of today and the reality of tomorrow." I also hope you will learn from history and be inspired, then look to the stars and dare to dream!

Future Mars explorers

TIME LINE

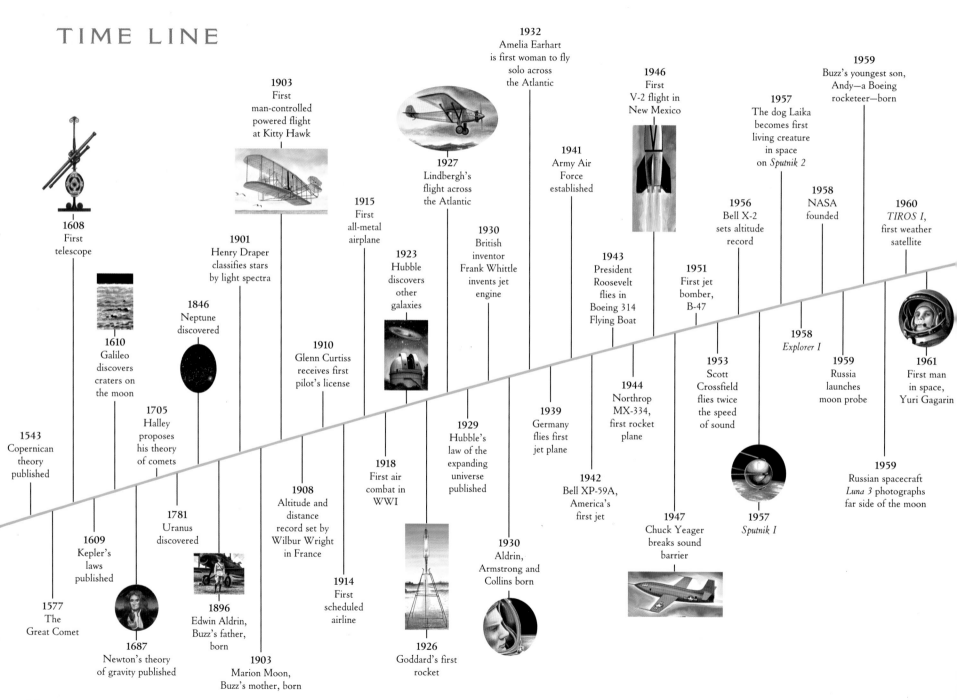

1543
Copernican theory published

1577
The Great Comet

1608
First telescope

1609
Kepler's laws published

1610
Galileo discovers craters on the moon

1687
Newton's theory of gravity published

1705
Halley proposes his theory of comets

1781
Uranus discovered

1846
Neptune discovered

1896
Edwin Aldrin, Buzz's father, born

1901
Henry Draper classifies stars by light spectra

1903
First man-controlled powered flight at Kitty Hawk

1903
Marion Moon, Buzz's mother, born

1908
Altitude and distance record set by Wilbur Wright in France

1910
Glenn Curtiss receives first pilot's license

1914
First scheduled airline

1915
First all-metal airplane

1918
First air combat in WWI

1923
Hubble discovers other galaxies

1926
Goddard's first rocket

1927
Lindbergh's flight across the Atlantic

1929
Hubble's law of the expanding universe published

1930
British inventor Frank Whittle invents jet engine

1930
Aldrin, Armstrong and Collins born

1932
Amelia Earhart is first woman to fly solo across the Atlantic

1939
Germany flies first jet plane

1941
Army Air Force established

1942
Bell XP-59A, America's first jet

1943
President Roosevelt flies in Boeing 314 Flying Boat

1944
Northrop MX-334, first rocket plane

1946
First V-2 flight in New Mexico

1947
Chuck Yeager breaks sound barrier

1951
First jet bomber, B-47

1953
Scott Crossfield flies twice the speed of sound

1956
Bell X-2 sets altitude record

1957
The dog Laika becomes first living creature in space on *Sputnik 2*

1957
Sputnik I

1958
NASA founded

1958
Explorer I

1959
Buzz's youngest son, Andy—a Boeing rocketeer—born

1959
Russia launches moon probe

1959
Russian spacecraft *Luna 3* photographs far side of the moon

1960
TIROS I, first weather satellite

1961
First man in space, Yuri Gagarin

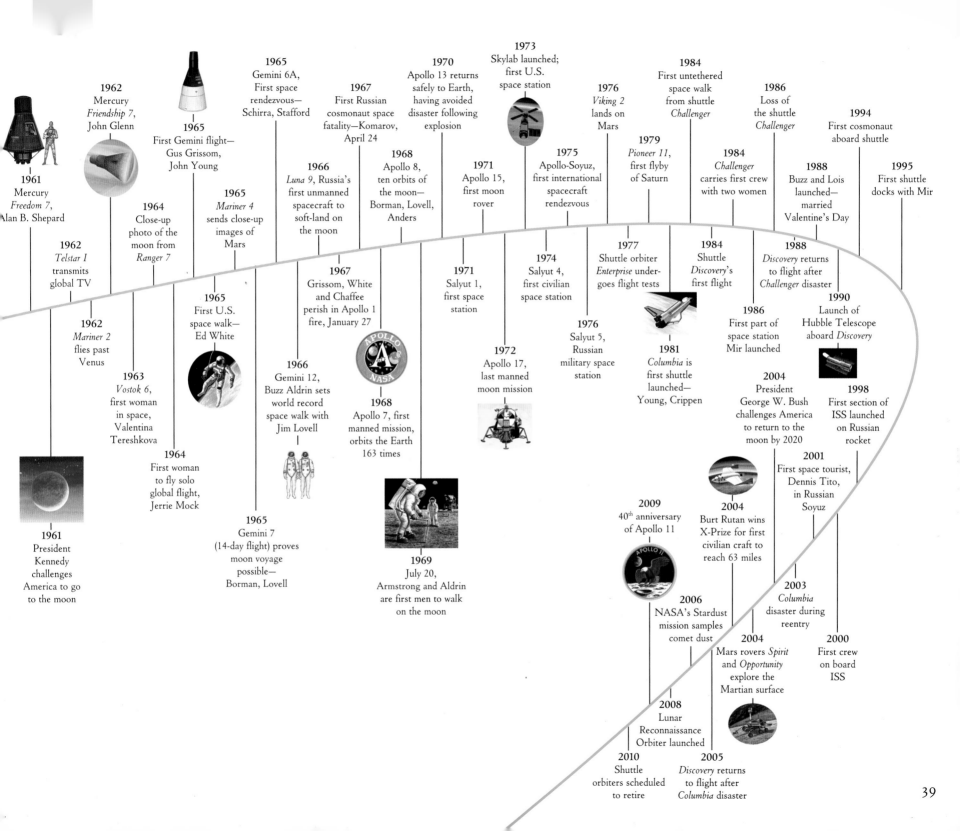

1961
Mercury
Freedom 7,
Alan B. Shepard

1961
President
Kennedy
challenges
America to go
to the moon

1962
Telstar I
transmits
global TV

1962
Mercury
Friendship 7,
John Glenn

1962
Mariner 2
flies past
Venus

1963
Vostok 6,
first woman
in space,
Valentina
Tereshkova

1964
Close-up
photo of the
moon from
Ranger 7

1964
First woman
to fly solo
global flight,
Jerrie Mock

1965
First Gemini flight—
Gus Grissom,
John Young

1965
Mariner 4
sends close-up
images of
Mars

1965
First U.S.
space walk—
Ed White

1965
Gemini 6A,
First space
rendezvous—
Schirra, Stafford

1965
Gemini 7
(14-day flight) proves
moon voyage
possible—
Borman, Lovell

1966
Luna 9, Russia's
first unmanned
spacecraft to
soft-land on
the moon

1966
Gemini 12,
Buzz Aldrin sets
world record
space walk with
Jim Lovell

1967
First Russian
cosmonaut space
fatality—Komarov,
April 24

1967
Grissom, White
and Chaffee
perish in Apollo 1
fire, January 27

1968
Apollo 8,
ten orbits of
the moon—
Borman, Lovell,
Anders

1968
Apollo 7, first
manned mission,
orbits the Earth
163 times

1969
July 20,
Armstrong and Aldrin
are first men to walk
on the moon

1970
Apollo 13 returns
safely to Earth,
having avoided
disaster following
explosion

1971
Apollo 15,
first moon
rover

1971
Salyut 1,
first space
station

1972
Apollo 17,
last manned
moon mission

1973
Skylab launched;
first U.S.
space station

1974
Salyut 4,
first civilian
space station

1975
Apollo-Soyuz,
first international
spacecraft
rendezvous

1976
Viking 2
lands on
Mars

1976
Salyut 5,
Russian
military space
station

1977
Shuttle orbiter
Enterprise under-
goes flight tests

1979
Pioneer 11,
first flyby
of Saturn

1981
Columbia is
first shuttle
launched—
Young, Crippen

1984
First untethered
space walk
from shuttle
Challenger

1984
Challenger
carries first crew
with two women

1984
Shuttle
Discovery's
first flight

1986
Loss of
the shuttle
Challenger

1986
First part of
space station
Mir launched

1988
Buzz and Lois
launched—
married
Valentine's Day

1988
Discovery returns
to flight after
Challenger disaster

1990
Launch of
Hubble Telescope
aboard *Discovery*

1994
First cosmonaut
aboard shuttle

1995
First shuttle
docks with Mir

1998
First section of
ISS launched
on Russian
rocket

2000
First crew
on board
ISS

2001
First space tourist,
Dennis Tito,
in Russian
Soyuz

2003
Columbia
disaster during
reentry

2004
President
George W. Bush
challenges America
to return to the
moon by 2020

2004
Burt Rutan wins
X-Prize for first
civilian craft to
reach 63 miles

2004
Mars rovers *Spirit*
and *Opportunity*
explore the
Martian surface

2005
Discovery returns
to flight after
Columbia disaster

2006
NASA's Stardust
mission samples
comet dust

2008
Lunar
Reconnaissance
Orbiter launched

2009
40th anniversary
of Apollo 11

2010
Shuttle
orbiters scheduled
to retire

39

SELECTED SOURCES

Aldrin, Buzz. "Roadmap to Mars." *Popular Mechanics,* December 2005, p. 64.

Aldrin, Buzz, and Malcolm McConnell. *Men from Earth*. New York: Bantam Books, 1989.

Aldrin, Buzz, with Wayne Warga. *Return to Earth*. New York: Random House, 1973.

De Goursac, Olivier. *Space: Exploring the Moon, the Planets, and Beyond*. New York: Abrams Books for Young Readers, 2006.

Dyson, Marianne J. *Home on the Moon: Living on a Space Frontier*. Washington, D.C.: National Geographic Society, 2003.

Gallant, Roy A. *National Geographic Picture Atlas of Our Universe*. Washington, D.C.: National Geographic Society, 1986.

Gorn, Michael. *NASA: The Complete Illustrated History*. London: Merrell Publishers, 2005.

Hughes, David, and Robin Kerrod. *Visual Encyclopedia of Space*. London: DK Publishing, 2006.

Man in Space: An Illustrated History from Sputnik to Columbia. *Life* Vol. 3, No. 3 (March 17, 2003).

National Geographic Encyclopedia of Space. Washington, D.C.: National Geographic Society, 2005.

Reynolds, David West. *Apollo: The Epic Journey to the Moon*. New York: Harcourt (A Tehabi Book), 2002.

Schorer, Lonnie Jones. *Kids to Space: A Space Traveler's Guide*. Burlington, Ont.: Apogee Books, 2006.

Stott, Carole. *Eyewitness Space Exploration*. New York: DK Publishing, 2004.

Wachhorst, Wyn. *The Dream of Spaceflight: Essays on the Near Edge of Infinity*. New York: Basic Books, 2000.

WEBSITES

NASA   www.nasa.gov

National Space Society   www.nss.org

ShareSpace Foundation   www.sharespace.org

American Astronautical Society   www.astronautical.org

The Moon Society   www.moonsociety.org

The Mars Society   www.marssociety.org

The Planetary Society   www.planetary.org

Space Tourism Society   www.spacetourismsociety.org

Aerospace Leadership   www.aiaa.org

SpaceShipOne   www.scaled.com

NASA Science for Kids   www.nasascience.nasa.gov/kids

NASA for Students   www.nasa.gov/audience/forstudents

Challenger Center   www.challenger.org

Amazing Space   amazing-space.stsci.edu

Astronomy for Kids   www.kidsastronomy.com

Space Place   spaceplace.nasa.gov

Buzz Aldrin   www.buzzaldrin.com

"Anyone who has spent any time in space will love it
for the rest of their lives."

—*Valentina Tereshkova, first woman in space*

"All adventures, especially into new territory, are scary."

—*Sally Ride, first American woman in space*

"I see Earth! It is so beautiful!"

—*Yuri Gagarin, first man in space*